What Is Sound?

Exploring Science with Hands-on Activities

Richard and Louise Spilsbury

Enslow Elementary

an imprint of

Enslow Publishers, Inc.
40 Industrial Road
Box 398
Berkeley Heights, NJ 07922
USA

http://www.enslow.com

Enslow Elementary, an imprint of Enslow Publishers, Inc.

Enslow Elementary® is a registered trademark of Enslow Publishers, Inc.

This edition published in 2008 by Enslow Publishers, Inc.

Library of Congress Cataloging-in-Publication Data

Spilsbury, Richard, 1963-
  What is sound? : exploring science with hands-on activities / Richard and Louise Spilsbury.
     p. cm. — (In touch with basic science)
  Summary: "An introduction to the properties of sound for third and fourth graders; includes hands-on activities"—Provided by publisher.
  Includes bibliographical references and index.
  ISBN-13: 978-0-7660-3098-5
  ISBN-10: 0-7660-3098-9
  1. Sound—Experiments—Juvenile literature. 2. Science—Experiments—Juvenile literature. 3. Science—Study and teaching—Activity programs—Juvenile literature.
  I. Spilsbury, Louise. II. Title.
   QC225.5.S67 2008
   534.078—dc22

                    2007024520

Printed in the United States of America

10 9 8 7 6 5 4 3 2 1

For The Brown Reference Group plc
Project Editor: Sarah Eason
Designer: Paul Myerscough
Picture Researcher: Maria Joannou
Managing Editor: Bridget Giles
Editorial Director: Lindsey Lowe
Production Director: Alastair Gourlay
Children's Publisher: Anne O'Daly

Photographic and Illustration Credits: Illustrations by Geoff Ward. Model Photography by Tudor Photography. Additional photographs from Corbis/Hugh Sitton/zefa, p. 18; istockphoto, p. 16; NASA, p. 6; Rex Features, p. 26; Shutterstock, pp. 4, 10.

Cover Photo: Tudor Photography

contents

WHAT IS SOUND?

Millions of different sounds can be made. Sounds can be as quiet as a whisper, or as loud as a speeding train. Sounds can be pleasant—or not. But what exactly is sound?

Sound is created when something vibrates in a particular way. If you hit a drum, you can hear the sound the vibration makes. You can also see the drum's surface vibrate. But most vibrations that create sound are too small to see.

Vibrations on the Move

When an object vibrates, the vibrations travel through the air. When the vibrations reach your ears, you hear them as sound. When the vibrations stop, the sound stops.

CLOSE-UP

SOUND MOVEMENT

When an object vibrates, it vibrates against air molecules around it. These molecules then vibrate against other air molecules, which then also vibrate. Imagine a row of dominoes standing on their ends. If you push the first domino, it will knock over the next domino and so on. Sound energy is passed on from one air molecule to another in the same way.

- **When you beat a drum, its surface vibrates. Air molecules around the drum then also vibrate. The vibrations pass through the air to reach our ears. That is how we hear sounds.**

If you put your hand on a drum to stop it from vibrating, you also stop the noise.

Solids, Liquids, and Gases

Sound can travel through gases, such as air. It can also travel through solids and liquids. Sound can travel through any object that can vibrate.

◀ *Both people and animals use sound to communicate. Dolphins use sound to communicate with each other underwater.*

Sound Waves

Sound vibrations move in curved up and down patterns. These movements are called sound waves. The size and speed of the sound waves determine what kind of sound is made.

Loud and Soft

Sounds can be loud or soft. Loud sounds are made by big vibrations. Big vibrations make tall sound waves. That is why a drum makes a louder sound when it is hit firmly than when it is hit gently. Soft or quiet sounds have much smaller vibrations and much smaller sound waves.

▼ *Did you know that it is completely silent in outer space? That is because there is no air for sounds to travel through!*

Why Sound Fades

Loud sounds can be heard from far away. But all sounds begin to fade soon after they are made, and can only travel a certain distance. That is because the sound wave keeps losing more and more energy as it crashes into the molecules in the air or other matter it is traveling through.

Sound spreads out in all directions. As sound spreads its vibrations get smaller. As the wave becomes smaller, the sound fades. Eventually the wave and the sound disappear altogether.

CLOSE-UP

HIGH AND LOW

When an object vibrates quickly, it makes a high sound, such as a squeak. When an object vibrates slowly, it makes a low sound, such as a hum. The number of vibrations per second is called frequency. Quick vibrations are called high frequency, and slow vibrations are called low frequency.

- A high-frequency vibration has many waves per second.

- A low-frequency vibration has few waves per second.

7

Bouncing Waves

Can a sound make an object move?
Try this experiment to find out.

1 Using your ruler and pen, draw lines across and down the cardboard to make a grid. Each square on your grid should be 2 inches (5 cm) long.

You will need

- large sheet of thick, white cardboard
- pen and pencil • ruler • balloon
- large can, open at both ends • mirror to fit on end of can • flashlight • tape
- strong glue • scissors • rubber band

SAFETY TIP

Ask an adult to cut the ends off the can and tape over any sharp edges.

2 Ask an adult to tape over any sharp points along the edges of the can. Cut off the open, narrow end of the balloon. Stretch the balloon over one end of the can. Secure the balloon to the can with the rubber band.

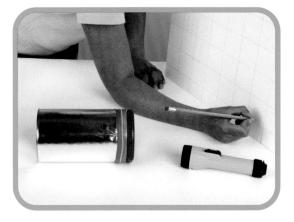

3 Glue the mirror to the balloon. Prop your cardboard against a pile of books, so that it stands up. Position the can and flashlight on the table, so that the light from the flashlight shines onto the mirror and reflects onto the card. The light should shine onto one square on the cardboard. Make a mark in that square.

4 Clap your hands together 6 inches (15 cm) behind the can. The light from the flashlight should move into another square. Make a mark in that square.

WHAT HAPPENED?

Sounds are made when objects vibrate, but sounds can also *make* objects vibrate. When you clapped your hands, sound waves traveled from your hands and hit the balloon. This made it move a little. When the balloon moved, the mirror also moved. These movements are tiny, so the flashlight was used to help show that the movement happened.

5 Measure the distance between the first and second marks you made. How far did the light jump?

9

THE SPEED OF SOUND

You have probably heard people talk about the speed of sound. This is the amount of time it takes sound to travel through the air. Sound travels through air at a speed of about 1,100 feet (330 m) per second.

Sounds in Air

Sound does not always travel through air at the same speed. Sound travels faster through dry air than through moist air. It also moves faster through warm air than it does through cold air. For instance, you would hear the sound of an airplane traveling in the sky much more quickly on a hot day than on a cool day.

"Supersonic" means "more than sound," or faster than the speed of sound. If a supersonic jet flies toward you, it will pass you before you hear it! But if your friend is laughing and running toward you, you will hear the laugh before your friend reaches you. ▶

CLOSE-UP

ECHO SOUNDERS

Ships use sound to calculate water depth. They also use sound to find objects underwater, such as schools of fish. A machine called an echo sounder sends sound waves to the bottom of the sea. When the sound waves hit the bottom (or another object), they bounce back. The depth can be figured out based on how long it takes for the sound waves to return to the ship.

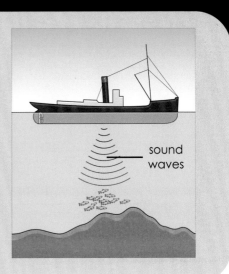

sound waves

Sound Speeds

Sound travels at different speeds through different materials. Sound travels about five times faster through water than through air. Sound travels faster through warmer water than through colder water.

Sound can travel very quickly in some solids. In metals, such as copper or steel, sound travels about 10 to 15 times faster than it does in air. Copper and other such materials have been used to make telephone cables for this reason.

Sound Speeds

Did you know that you can measure the speed at which sound travels? Follow these steps to discover how.

You will need

- measuring tape • an outside wall (with a large empty space around it)
- piece of chalk • metal trashcan lid
- spoon • stopwatch

1 Use the measuring tape to measure a distance of 150 feet (45 m) from the wall. Head directly away from the wall in a straight line.

2 Mark the distance on the ground with the chalk. Carefully measure the same distance again. Make another chalk mark. If your two marks are not in the same place, draw a line halfway between them. By measuring the distance twice, you are more likely to get an accurate measurement than by measuring just once.

3 Stand next to a friend on the chalk mark. You should both face the wall. One person should bang on the trashcan lid with the spoon. One person should start the stopwatch as the trashcan lid is hit.

4 When you hear the echo of the noise made by the lid and spoon, hit the trashcan lid again. Try to hit the lid so that the second bang occurs at the same time as the echo from the first bang. Repeat this 20 times. Stop the watch after you hear the twentieth echo. Record the time.

WHAT HAPPENED?

The distance to the wall and back is 150 feet + 150 feet, or 300 feet (90 m). You measured the time it took for the sound to travel to the wall and back 20 times. The total distance it traveled was 20 x 300 feet, or 6,000 feet (2,000 m).

To figure out speed, divide the distance the sound traveled by the time it took to travel. Divide the 6,000 feet by the total time in seconds that you recorded. Your answer will be in feet per seconds. The average speed of sound is 1,100 feet per second. What was your answer?

Try this!

Scientists often repeat their experiments several times to improve accuracy. What results do you get if you try this experiment again?

Slow Down Sound

Can you make sound waves travel more slowly? Try this activity to find out.

1 Use the funnel to put the baking powder into the bottle. Add the vinegar. You might hear or see fizzing when the powder and vinegar mix. This is because a gas called carbon dioxide (CO_2) is being created.

2 Quickly stretch the balloon over the neck of the bottle. The carbon dioxide gas should enter the balloon and begin to inflate it.

You will need

- plastic bottle with a narrow neck
- funnel • tablespoon • 2 tablespoons of baking powder • 2 tablespoons of vinegar • balloon • string and tape
- saucer • radio

3 When the balloon is fully inflated, use some string to tie the neck of the balloon tight. Next, use some tape to firmly attach the balloon to the saucer. The balloon should not move.

4 Put the radio about 1.5 feet (45 cm) in front of the balloon. Switch the radio on and turn up the volume—but not too loud! Put your ear to the other side of the balloon. Keep moving your head around the balloon until you find the point where the sound is loudest. Cover your other ear. Ask someone to turn down the volume of the radio until you can only just hear it.

5 Now remove the balloon. Does the radio sound louder or quieter?

WHAT HAPPENED?

Carbon dioxide is denser than air. The sound waves took longer to travel through the carbon dioxide in the balloon than through the air outside the balloon. That concentrated the sound inside the balloon, which is why the radio sounded louder through the balloon.

Also, the sound waves bent inward when they passed through the curved sides of the balloon. That also focused the sound by your ear, making the radio sound louder.

Try this!

Try the listening test again, but this time with a helium-filled balloon. Helium is lighter than air. That is why helium balloons float in air. Did the helium balloon make the radio sounds quieter or louder? Are the sounds higher or lower?

RESONANCE

Remember that sound causes objects to vibrate. When one object vibrates at the same speed as another nearby object, the sound made by each object is increased. This effect is called resonance.

An object can vibrate at different speeds, but every object has one or more speeds at which it is most likely to vibrate. That is the object's resonant frequency.

Different objects have different resonant frequencies. The rate depends on the type and the amount of material the object is made from. For example, wood vibrates at a different frequency than glass, and small objects vibrate more quickly than large objects.

Standing Waves

If you blow into a recorder or a flute, sound waves move from the mouthpiece to the end of the

▼ *When you beat a gong over and over again, sounds at its resonant frequency build up. This makes the sound get louder and louder.*

CLOSE-UP

GLASS RESONANCE

When you rub your finger along the top rim of a wineglass, it causes the rim to move in and out. If you rub the glass for a long time, the speed at which the rim moves in and out begins to match the natural speed at which the glass vibrates. That creates resonance. The movements of the glass also make the air inside and around the glass vibrate more quickly. The air vibrates most quickly at the rim of the glass, which is where sound waves from the glass and air meet to create a standing wave. That creates the sound you hear when you rub a wineglass.

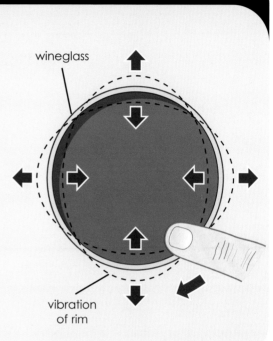

wineglass

vibration
of rim

instrument and back again. When you pluck a string, sound waves travel back and forth along the string's length. When a forward-moving wave meets a backward-moving wave, they join to make a sound wave that seems to stand still.

Standing waves are most likely to form in the part of an instrument that vibrates the strongest, where the sound the instrument makes is loudest. That helps to create the strong, loud note you hear when the instrument is played.

CHANGING NOTES

A piece of music has lots of different notes, or pitches. Different pitches have different frequencies of sound waves. High pitches are made by sound waves at faster frequencies, and low pitches are made by sound waves at slower frequencies.

Different Pitches

How do musicians change notes as they play? Different instruments usually resonate at different pitches. Some instruments, such as a drum, can make just one pitch. The long strings of a double bass produce standing waves at a lower pitch than the shorter strings of a violin. That is why different instruments are often used to play different parts of a piece of music.

◄ *The panpipe has tubes of different lengths. A musician changes pitch by blowing over different tubes. The air inside each tube resonates at a different frequency.*

Changing Pitch

We can change the pitch of music by playing different parts of an instrument. We can also change pitch by using our fingers. For example, when we cover more holes on a recorder or flute, we increase the distance sound waves can move inside the instrument. The air then resonates at a lower pitch.

When Sound Waves Meet

When the sound waves of two identical pitches meet, their frequencies can join. This either makes one loud sound wave, or cancels out both sound waves. However, when two slightly different pitches meet, they make a new sound wave. We hear this wave as a sound that goes from loud to soft to loud and so on. The regular changes of volume are called beats.

CLOSE-UP

STRINGS AND FINGERS

Pressing a string against the neck of a guitar shortens the length of string that can resonate. When you pluck the string, you create a standing wave of higher pitch than when the string is at its usual length. That is because vibrations travel a shorter distance. Moving your finger farther toward the wide part of the guitar shortens the string even more, and makes an even higher pitch.

● **Longer distance for waves to travel = lower pitch.**

● **Shorter distance for waves to travel = higher pitch.**

19

Standing Waves

Can more than one standing wave occur in an object? Follow these steps to find out.

1 Hold the tube in the bucket of water with just one hand. Just the top of the tube should be seen above the water.

You will need
- bucket of water (about two-thirds full)
- long plastic tube 1 inch (27 mm) wide, open at both ends • pen • tuning fork (you can buy a tuning fork from a music shop)

2 With the other hand, strike the tuning fork on a table top to make its prongs vibrate.

3 Hold the fork just above the end of the tube. With your other hand, slowly lift the tube out of the water. Keep the fork just above the tube opening and keep listening!

4 You should find a point at which the tuning fork sounds especially loud. Mark where the water level is on the tube.

Try this!

Repeat the experiment, but this time use tuning forks of different sizes. Do the standing waves occur in the same places that you marked on the tube in the original experiment?

WHAT HAPPENED?

When you lifted the tube from the water, more of the tube was able to resonate. That made the air inside the tube vibrate at a lower frequency, until it matched the fork's frequency. At this point the sound waves inside the tube were loudest because a standing wave had formed.

Like water waves, sound waves repeat themselves over and over again. In a long tube standing waves will form in several places. The second loud spot you found by raising your tube was caused by another standing wave.

5 Put the tube back into the bucket of water. Repeat the activity to see if there is a different point on the tube where the sound gets louder.

String Sounds

How can you change an instrument to make its pitch higher or lower? Try this activity to find out.

1 Have an adult twist one hook into the bottom of the can. It should be 1–2 inches (2.5–5 cm) from one edge of the can.

SAFETY TIP

Make sure an adult screws the hooks into the can.

You will need
- large, empty can
- two screw hooks
- modeling clay
- ruler
- thin elastic
- small plastic bottle
- metal nuts or identical coins

2 Use modeling clay to attach the ruler to the opposite edge of the can, so it stands on one of its long edges. Cut a piece of elastic and tie one end around the hook. Tie the other end of the elastic to the bottle.

3 Place the can by the table edge. Drop a few nuts or coins into the bottle and hang it over the table edge. The elastic between the hook and the bottle should go over the ruler. Pluck the elastic just behind the ruler. Listen to the note it makes.

4 Repeat this activity several times, putting two more nuts or coins into the bottle each time. How does the pitch change as the weight in the bottle increases?

5 Have an adult screw the second hook into the bottom of the can near to the ruler. Tie the elastic and bottle to this hook. Pluck the elastic just behind the ruler. How does this pitch compare to the one using the first hook?

WHAT HAPPENED?

When you added weight to the bottle, you increased the tension of the elastic. Increasing the tension of the elastic made its pitch higher. When you used the second hook, you made the elastic shorter. The elastic should then have made an even higher pitch.

Try this!

Repeat the experiment using both thick, heavy elastic and very thin, light elastic. Does the material a string is made from change its pitch, even if the length of the string remains the same?

Create a Beat!

Can you make beats with sound?
Follow the steps to find out.

You will need
- two identical slide whistles (whistles with a movable piston, or stick, that changes the pitch) • 1-foot (30-cm) ruler • stopwatch or wristwatch with a second hand

1 Pull the piston of each whistle halfway out of the whistle. Ask a friend to blow into their whistle with an even and steady breath. They should keep blowing at the same pitch. Now blow your whistle. Move the piston of your whistle until the pitch sounds the same as your friend's whistle.

2 Slowly pull out your whistle's piston. The sound beats from the two whistles should change from loud to soft. If you pull your piston even farther, the beats should become quicker and quicker, until you can no longer hear them.

3 Repeat step one. When the pitch of each whistle is the same, stop blowing and measure the length of both pistons.

WHAT HAPPENED?

You should have heard no beat when the two pistons were the same length.

Increasing the length of one whistle's piston made its pitch slightly different than the first whistle. The different frequencies from each whistle's pitch mixed. That made the sound beats.

By increasing the pistons' lengths, you made the pitches more varied and the beats faster.

You timed how long it took to hear 10 beats. Divide that number by 10 to find out how long each beat lasted. You should have found that increasing the piston length made each beat quicker.

4 Repeat step two. Ask someone to start the stopwatch at the point the beats are loudest. Stop pulling the piston at this point. Record the time it takes to hear 10 beats. Measure the piston's length.

WHAT CAN PEOPLE DO ABOUT NOISE?

Some noises are good, but some are unwanted. Even pleasant sounds, such as music, could be unwanted if they occur in the wrong place or at the wrong time.

Some noises, such as a jet taking off, can be a problem for people living nearby. Such noises are unlikely to stop. But people have found ways to reduce such unwanted sounds.

Reflecting Sounds

Sound waves are weakened when they reflect, or bounce, off a surface such as a wall. Large banks of earth or concrete walls are sometimes built alongside highways to reduce traffic noise. The banks reflect some of the traffic noise away from people's homes.

CLOSE-UP

REDUCING SOUND ENERGY

Sound waves travel at different rates through different materials. Some materials absorb sound energy. As the sound energy passes through the material, friction between the sound and the material changes some of the sound energy into a small amount of heat energy. That is how the material that the sound travels through reduces the sound.

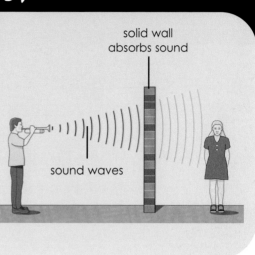

solid wall absorbs sound

sound waves

◀ *Loud noises can damage ears. People who work in noisy places, such as airports, usually wear ear protectors. The protectors reduce the amount of noise the wearer hears.*

Sound Insulation

Some materials soak up sound in the same way that a towel soaks up water. Other materials can soak up heat or electricity. We call these materials insulation. When insulation is put around the sources of noise, some of the noise can be blocked.

Insulation can also be put around an area to protect it from noise. For example, people who live near airports usually have double glazed windows. These windows have two panes of glass that trap a layer of air between them. The layer of air absorbs sound and reduces the noise of overhead planes.

27

Sound Insulation

Did you know that some materials provide more sound insulation than others? Try this experiment to discover why.

You will need

- small radio • cardboard • padded envelopes • bubble wrap • Styrofoam™ • tape • cushion or pillow • ruler • scissors

1 Cut the cardboard, envelopes, bubble wrap, and Styrofoam into a shape that can be used to cover the radio's speaker. Each shape should extend about 0.5 inches (1.5 cm) beyond the edges of the radio speaker.

2 Each piece of material should be at least 0.5 inches (1.30 cm) thick. If a piece is too thin, cut out several more pieces. Tape the pieces together, one on top of the other, until the shape is 0.5 inches (1.30 cm) thick.

WHAT HAPPENED?

You should have found that some materials provide more insulation (block sound) than others. Denser materials, such as Styrofoam, absorb more sound than less dense materials, such as paper. Materials that are soft, such as a cushion, usually absorb more sound than hard materials, such as cardboard.

3 Turn on the radio and lay it face up on the cushion or pillow. (The cushion will absorb any sound that might come from the back of the radio.) Place a piece of material over the radio speaker. Slowly turn down the volume button and listen to the radio. Stop turning when you can no longer hear the sound. Read the number on the volume scale. Write the number next to the name of the material you tested.

4 Repeat the experiment with each piece of material. Remember to record the number on the volume scale next to the name of the material.

Try this!

Make each piece of material thicker and repeat the experiment. What difference does the thickness of the insulation make to the volume of the sound?

GLOSSARY

beat—When two slightly different pitches combine to make a regular, pulsing sound.

echo—Reflected sound wave. An echo repeats a sound a few seconds after it has been made.

energy—Ability to do work, such as to make something move or change.

frequency—Speed at which a sound wave vibrates.

insulation—Material that slows or blocks the movement of sound, heat, or electricity.

pitch—How high or low a sound is, determined by the frequency of the waves producing it.

resonance—When an object vibrates at the same speed as another nearby object.

resonant frequency—Frequency at which an object naturally tends to vibrate.

sound wave—Invisible up-and-down curved pattern of movement of sound energy through the air.

standing wave—When two waves of the same frequency, but traveling in opposite directions, meet.

supersonic—Faster than the speed of sound.

tension—Force that pulls or stretches.

vibrate—To move in regular motions backward and forward.

FURTHER READING

Books

Johnson, Rececca L. *The Magic of Light and Sound*. Washington D.C.: National Geographic Society (2003).

Parker, Steve. *The Science of Sound: Projects and Experiments with Music and Sound Waves*. Chicago, Ill.: Heinemann (2005).

Tocci, Salvatore. *Experiments with Sound*. New York: Children's Press (2001).

Internet Addresses

Science of Sound: Activities
http://www.smm.org/sound/nocss/activity/top.html

Exploratorium
http://www.exploratorium.edu/music/

Science Clips
www.bbc.co.uk/schools/scienceclips/ages/9_10/changing_sounds.shtml

INDEX